MW01077533

Just for Journaling
Holidays & Seasons

Created & Designed by Dianne J. Hook
Creative Journaling Templates for Classroom & Home

ISBN:1-59441-004-6

Contents

Credits

Illustrator: Dianne J. Hook
Content Design
   and Project Director: Sherrill B. Flora
Editor: Karen Seberg
Production: Mark Conrad
Cover Production: Annette Hollister-Papp

Introduction to Creative Journal Writing
with the Fun of Decorative Templates

Here are some creative suggestions
for holiday and seasonal journal writing experiences.

The Purpose of Journals in the Classroom

Journal writing has become increasingly important in today's curriculum. As a teacher, you can make journal writing fun and exciting by providing your students with motivational and creative writing ideas. *Just for Journaling: Holidays & Seasons* offers over 60 pages of delightful illustrations that will motivate and encourage your young writers.

Journals have many important educational purposes. They can be one of several tools used to evaluate student learning; they can provide regular information about a student's writing; and they can also help students learn to express their thoughts. Journal writing is most effective when used as a regular activity throughout the school week. The length of each session may vary from 10 to 20 minutes, depending on the age of your students. Provide the students with several copies of journal writing paper. Use the instructions below to create journal paper that changes with the seasons and holidays.

Assembly Instructions for Creating a Journal Page with a Lined-Handwriting Template

1. Lined-handwriting templates can be found on pages 4, 5, and 6 of this book. Choose the template that is the most appropriate for the writing abilities of your students. Then, select a decorative seasonal or holiday border page.

2. Make copies of the lined-handwriting template and border of your choice. Cut the lined-handwriting template to fit inside the border. Use blue grid paper or a light table to make sure that you have properly centered the writing lines. Attach the template to the inside of the border with doublestick tape or rubber cement.

3. Try to keep a ¼-inch margin on all edges of your paper. If the cutting edges from the lined-handwriting template are visible on your first copy, lighten the copy machine setting by one notch. Alternatively, use correction fluid on the first copy, and then use that copy to make the final journal pages for your students.

Have fun! Your classroom of students will become eager writers
with the adorable pages from *Just for Journaling: Holidays & Seasons*.

Pinecone Moose

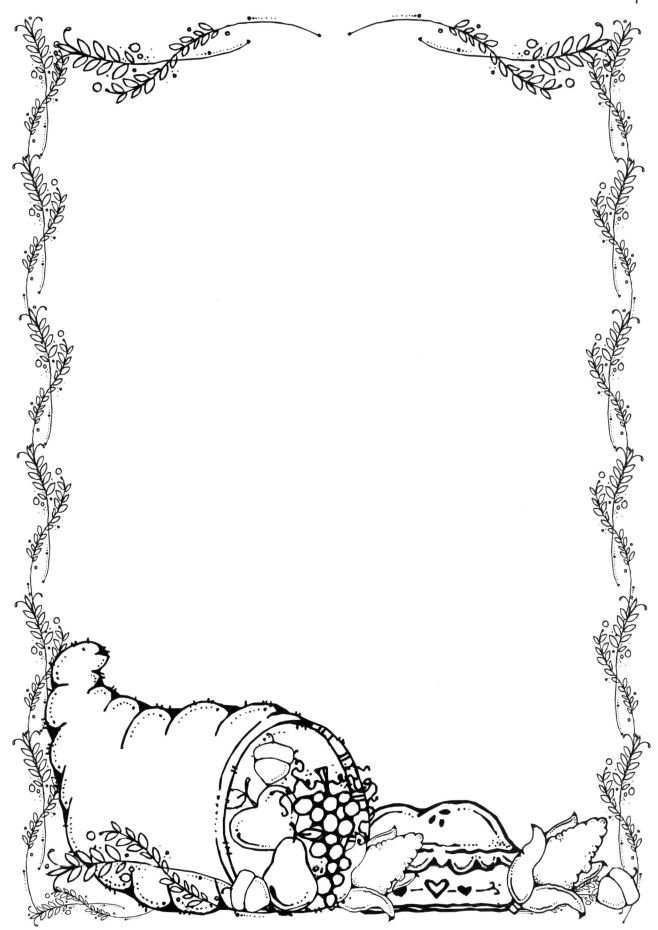

Polar Pals

31

Happy Hanukkah

Happy Hanukkah

FOR YOU

Spring Bunny

Baby Ducks

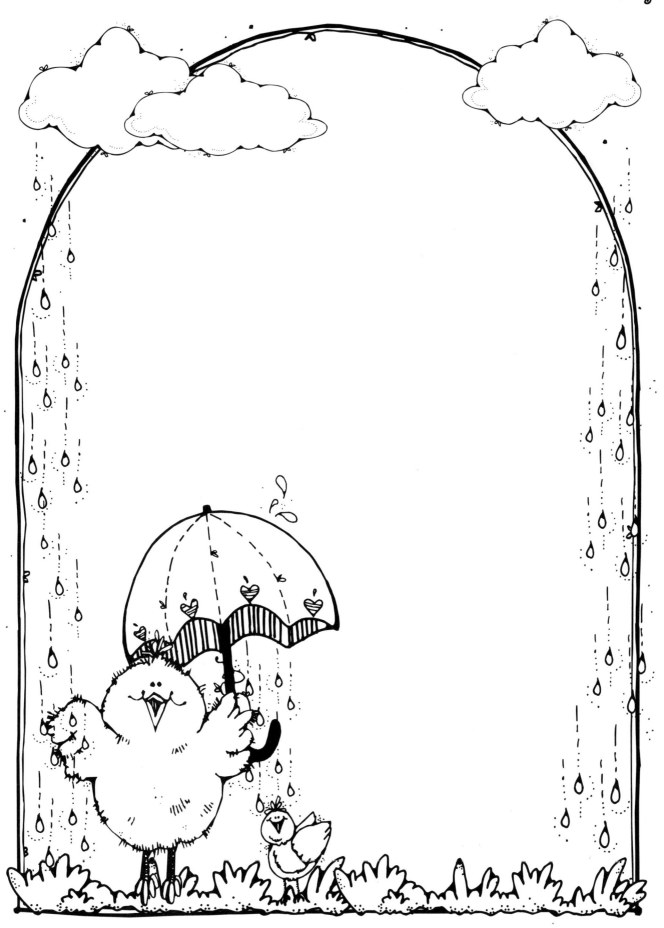

Rainbow

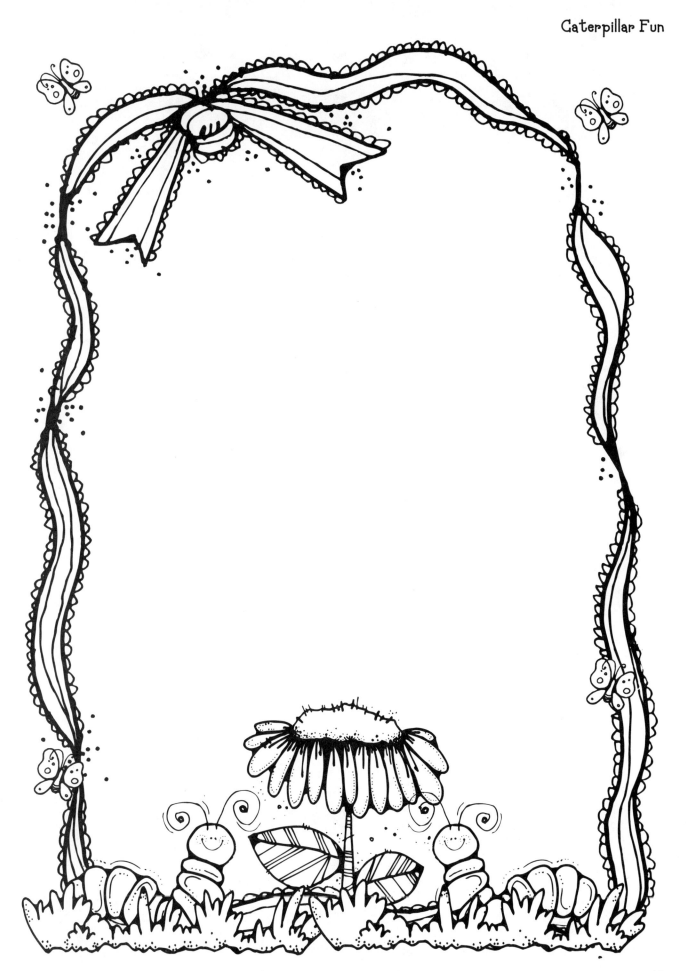